the Mystery of Knowing

Journal

A writing odyssey to be
true to who you are

Sarri Gilman, LMFT

Other books by Sarri Gilman

Transform Your Boundaries
Naming and Taming Overwhelm for Healthcare and Human Service Providers

Classes by the author are available online at Teachable.

The Mystery of Knowing Journal / by Sarri Gilman
ISBN-13: 978-0-9897787-6-3

Island Bound Publishing
SarriGilman.com

Designed & Illustrated by Tarsha Rockowitz
trockdesign.com

Dear Writer,

I created this guided journal to support you as you dive deeply into a reflecting process through writing. While teaching workshops about self-care, boundaries, and recovering from overwhelm, I learned that very few people attending my workshops had a journal practice.

Though you can learn things from my books and workshops, as well as from those offered by others, your greatest learning will come from inside of you. Journaling is an inside-out, individual process.

A journal practice can help you take down the walls that stop you from knowing yourself. It's time to reveal who you really are.

You may feel exposed and vulnerable for a bit, but you will also feel more intimate with yourself and eventually with others.

My hope is you will discover, through writing, ways to nurture your spirit and be true to who you are.

Maybe you have not had time to sit with a journal. Perhaps you aren't sure how a journal could help you exercise self-care, experience more joy, and grow healthy boundaries. If you are new to journaling, I only want you to spend ten minutes in this journal when you write. Short bursts of writing.

I am often asked how to use a journal to dive in deeper, below the surface, and get to the heart of things. The questions in this journal will guide you below the surface. The questions will start you on a trail. Where the trail leads is what you will discover as you write.

Write inside the pages of this book. Think of your journal as your home, a place you come to and go from. When you open your journal, you are inside of the journal and also inside of yourself, your true home.

I am excited you are taking this journey.

Take good care of you,

Sarri Gilman,
Whidbey Island, Washington

Contents

How to Use The Mystery of Knowing Journal

I recommend you start at the beginning. There are many seeds planted in this book.
Go in order from page to page.

Make journal time comfortable and quiet. Journals like quiet places. It is hard to go below the surface when there are distractions.

Take your journal outside in nature and note what nature offers you as you write. A raven call, a feather, a moon shell—use whatever is offered as a gift in your writing.

Set up some boundaries so you won't be interrupted when you are journaling.

Get into a comfortable seat. Pour yourself a cup of something warm.
Be with yourself.
Use your favorite pen.

Go slowly through the pages, maybe one exercise every day or every few days. Spend ten to fifteen minutes on each writing exercise. Reread what you wrote in the exercise. Then always write a reflection about what you noticed.

Don't edit or cross anything out that comes to the page.
This rule is very important. You don't need to be perfect when you journal. You are practicing acceptance of yourself, your ideas, your mistakes, everything.

To hear your deep truth when you write, you can't edit yourself. Let messy stuff come to the page. If you wrote something and you want to clarify or change, just keep writing whatever you need to say. This part of the process teaches us to be accepting of ourselves. You are enough.

Some of the exercises you will return to again and again. All of the journal prompts are listed at the end of the book, and you can return to do the questions again. I'll explain why you will want to do that later, near the end, after you have finished your first round through this journal.

There are also collage prompts in this journal. Collaging is another way to express yourself and reflect. When you get to a collage prompt, you will make a collage using only two to four images and then write about your collages.

If you want to share the experience, you can invite others to grab their own copy of The Mystery of Knowing Journal and meet weekly to share insight and seeds.

Be True To Who You Are

Take your journal outside
and note what nature offers you as
you write. A raven call, a feather,
a moon shell, a stone—use whatever
is offered as a gift in your writing.

Follow the Prompts:

 Journal Prompt

 Collage Prompt

Self-Reflection

Self-reflection is a way of listening to yourself.

Most of what we hear from our minds is noise. My mind likes to make lists of things to do, stuff I forgot, or stuff I am worried I will forget, as well as echoes of conversations I may have had earlier in the day, notes I need to send, etc. It is shallow thinking. Nothing very interesting.

Journaling allows you to get below the surface.
You can make contact with your soul, your inner compass, your wisdom.

Your soul has many important things to share with you about your life.
Your inner compass is a teacher.

The best way to learn from your compass is to spend time journaling.

When you write in this journal, give yourself ten to fifteen minutes each time you write.

The process is:

WRITE *for ten to fifteen minutes*

READ *what you wrote*

REFLECT. *write a brief reflection about what you wrote*

Always do all three steps. Sometimes something new pops onto the page when you write the reflection. Self-reflection is a practice.

More about the Prompts

All of these exercises will have a journal prompt to help you get started on your writing journey. Look for the journal prompt icon to get you started.

And, remember to ALWAYS Read what you wrote and Reflect.

Let's get started!

I bought this journal because...

_____

_____

_____

_____

_____

_____

_____

_____

_____

_____

_____

_____

_____

_____

_____

Collaging is a way of speaking with images. Using images torn from a magazine can help us say something without words. When your collage is done, you can write about what you notice in your collage and how it relates to the issue, question, or topic you are journaling.

I collect magazines and old art books from library sales, thrift stores, friends, and garage sales.
I keep a big stack around at all times.
I use UHU Stic Glue Sticks and scissors.

How to write from a collage:

After you make a collage, write what you see in the collage.
You can start by writing a list of words that come to mind.
Keep listing until a thought comes through to the page.

I wrote this from a collage that had the night sky in the background with a couple embracing. It was after one person in the couple had passed away.

- Stars
- Moon
- Night sky
- Quiet
- Lovebirds
- Coupling
- Heaven
- Heaven holds the lovers in the night sky
- Eternal as the stars

Another way of writing from a collage is to use the journal prompt provided for your collage.

A Safe Place

A journal is a private conversation with your soul.

Your journal needs to have boundaries around it. All journal writing needs protection and safety. By keeping this journal in a safe, protected place, you will control what gets shared from it and with whom.

You never have to share what is in this journal. It belongs to you.

Where can you keep this journal safe and protected?

Imagine a bear is guarding your journal.

 Make a list of boundaries you want regarding your journal.

Authenticity

We have lots of ways to cover up our authentic selves.

When you journal, you can hear your deepest truth.

I call it your soul voice.

You may think of it as your gut, your truth, your wisdom, or your intuition.

Whatever you name this part of you, it is authentic.

As fast as you can, write a list of reasons why you want to be more connected to your authentic voice.

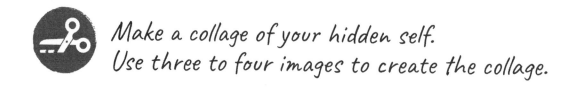

Make a collage of your hidden self.
Use three to four images to create the collage.

What do you see in your collage? Write a letter to your hidden self. Dear Hidden Self,

*Squirrels are good
at hiding things.*

Connection

Intimacy comes from sharing your deep truth with another person. When that part of you is hidden, no one really knows you. You may not really know yourself.

Being authentic is brave. It is the only path to closeness and connection.

Understanding your truth, your boundaries, and sharing that with others creates intimacy

 Who in your life, now or in the past, accepts you as you are and encourages you to be authentic?

My fear about being authentic is:

Boundary Card Bonus Activity

Look for the boundary cards sprinkled throughout this journal and use them as cues to practice boundary setting throughout your day.

 BOUNDARY CARD:

Use your Yes and No to lower your stress and protect yourself from overwhelm.

Courage

Working on your boundaries takes courage. You are going to dig inside of yourself and hear things that will challenge you. You will hear things that you wish weren't true. You will hear things that scare you.

Writing your way to your heart takes courage.

In what ways are you courageous?
What courageous things have you done?

Your Boundary Compass

Your boundaries are made of Yes and No. You have a compass inside of you where you decide what is a Yes and what is a No for you.

 Draw a picture or make a collage of your compass. Your compass has a Yes and No on it.

As you make a picture of your compass, think about these questions:

· Is it easier to say Yes than to say No?
· Are you able to say No and stick to it?
· Are you kind and calm when you say No or do you agonize over saying No?
· Are you listening to your callings, your Yeses? Or do these sound too crazy to you?
· Are you going after your dreams?
· Do you feel too busy?

How well do you listen to your true Yes and No?
When is it easy to listen? What makes it hard?

⬆ BOUNDARY CARD:

*You may fear setting boundaries
because you want approval.
Give yourself approval to say
Yes and No.*

Shoulds

When you are dealing with an issue in your life, you may hear a lot of "Shoulds" in your head. You Should do this, you Should do that.

 Make a bubble brainstorm of all the **Shoulds** you hear in your head. *(Illustration to help get you started)*

Make a collage of the *Shoulds* in your head.

You should....   You should....   You should....   You should....   You should....   You should....   You should....

You Should....

You should....

You should....

You should....

You should....

You should....

You should....

You should....   You should....   You should....   You should....   You should....   You should....   You should....

Find one image in a magazine to be the "Should speaker" in your head. Glue your Should speaker image here.

You should.... You should.... You should.... You should.... You should.... should.... You should....

Being Kind to Yourself

You can take care of yourself in many different ways. The first step to taking better of care of yourself is **being kind to yourself**.

When someone hurts your feelings, listen to your hurt feelings. You can write them down. You can close your eyes and feel your emotional pain.

Know that this pain is normal. People hurt each other. When this happens, say something kind to yourself and do something kind for yourself.

 Write some kind things you can say to yourself when you are hurting. Then read these words aloud to yourself. (When you are really hurting or upset, return to this JP.)

Make a collage (using only two to three images) of a Compassionate Being who is going to live in your heart.

Finish these sentences as if the Compassionate Being you created is talking to you:

I want you to know, you are... _____

_____

_____

I see... _____

_____

_____

My words for you are... _____

_____

_____

Trust... _____

_____

_____

When you are hurting in your heart... _____

_____

_____

_____

_____

_____

_____

What would you do?

What fun things would you do if you had more time?

 Writing as fast as you can, make a list of fifty fun things you would do if you had more time. (Pretend that money does not matter—list all the fun things you would like to do.) It's OK if you repeat yourself.

1. _____
2. _____
3. _____
4. _____
5. _____
6. _____
7. _____
8. _____
9. _____
10. _____
11. _____
12. _____
13. _____
14. _____
15. _____
16. _____
17. _____
18. _____
19. _____
20. _____
21. _____
22. _____
23. _____
24. _____

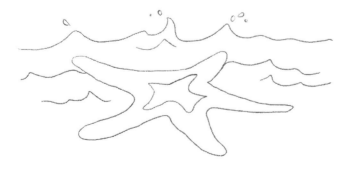

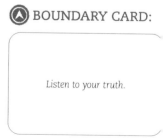

⬛ BOUNDARY CARD:

Listen to your truth.

25. _____
26. _____
27. _____
28. _____
29. _____
30. _____
31. _____
32. _____
33. _____
34. _____
35. _____
36. _____
37. _____

38. _____
39. _____
40. _____
41. _____
42. _____
43. _____
44. _____
45. _____
46. _____
47. _____
48. _____
49. _____
50. _____

_____
_____
_____
_____
_____
_____
_____
_____
_____
_____
_____
_____

Fun Things

Doing fun things is a big part of self-care. *Pick something from your list of fun things that you can make time to do this week.*

Keep adding to the list and write one fun thing you can do each day.

 You will need magazines, scissors, a large piece of paper, and a glue stick. Make a collage on a large piece of paper. This will be a vision board of the bigger fun things on your list.

(You can watch YouTube videos on vision boards to see examples.)

Is there something you need to learn? Or a supply you need? Or something you need to save up for? What will it take to go for your bigger fun? Put images of some of the fun things from your list. Put this collage somewhere you can see it. Take a picture of it and keep it on your phone to look at.

 Write some baby steps you can take now to help you get closer to these fun things.

Baby Steps

When you do something new, always do it in baby steps. Break it down into one small step at a time. It makes things less overwhelming.

I can try baby stepping with...

Write the steps you need to take.

Self-Care Wheel

There are many ways to take care of you. By creating a self-care wheel, you will see all the ways you can take care of yourself.

 Divide this circle into six sections.

Section 1.

Write FOUNDATION.
Your foundation of self-care is Eat, Sleep, Exercise.
Check in with yourself to see if you need to focus on your foundation.

Section 2.

Write FUN.
What do you like to do? Or what would you like to do for fun?

Section 3.

Write CREATIVE.
What do you enjoy doing that is creative?

Section 4.

Write PEACEFUL, QUIET, SPIRITUAL.
What do you like to do to experience peace, quiet, or spiritual connection?

Section 5.

Write SOCIAL.
Who would you like to spend more time with?
Friends and rich relationships are essential for your well-being.

Section 6.

Write EMOTIONAL.
How do you take care of your feelings?

Examples of Self-Care Wheels

Every year starting in January, make a new self-care wheel. You will notice that what you choose for self-care will change from year to year. The wheel allows you to ask yourself the question and then make a plan for your self-care.

Look closely at your wheel. It's OK to start anywhere. You are not going to do everything at once. You are going to pick one thing to start doing right now to improve your self-care.

Fill the slices with as many things that come to mind.

start here

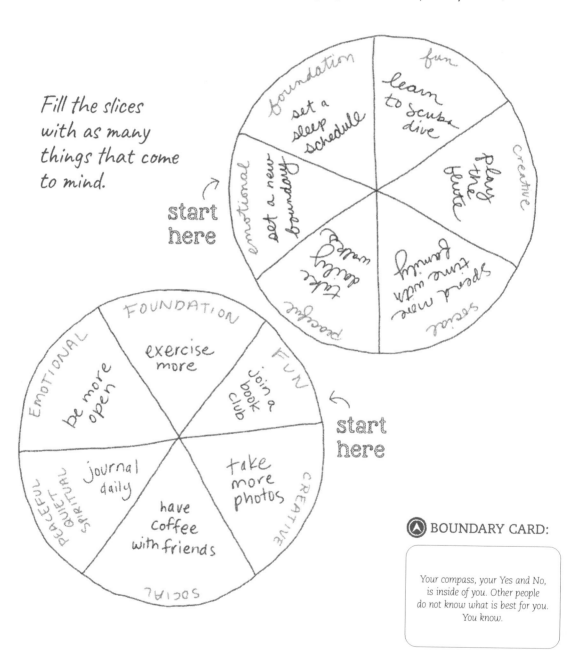

⬆ BOUNDARY CARD:

Your compass, your Yes and No, is inside of you. Other people do not know what is best for you. You know.

Which part of your self-care wheel is a good place to start improving your self-care? Why is that a good place for you to start?

Time and Your Self-Care

You are probably great at taking care of others. Making time to fill yourself and nurture yourself may take some practice. Start by devoting fifteen to twenty minutes each day for your self-care. This is time that feeds your soul, feels nurturing. You don't have to **DO** anything, you can just **BE**.

How can you wake from hibernation like the bear? What self-care needs is it time for you to wake up to?

Is self-care part of your daily plan? Is it written in your planner, your schedule, and your calendar? Be sure you have it in your calendar—this is an appointment with yourself.

Your time is a precious resource. You wake up each day, and time is what belongs to you. It may not feel like it belongs to you, but it does. You don't have to use every minute of it earning money or taking care of others.

Go ahead and claim some time for you. Put those dates with yourself in your calendar and then keep those dates.

Notice during the day and week the things that you are doing that waste your time. Making more time for self-care means skipping things that are time wasting.

Starfish tend to cling to things in the water. What could you stop clinging to that wastes your time?

Sleep

Going into your cave to sleep is a foundational part of self-care.
Your body is designed for seven to eight hours of nightly sleep.

Start by finishing this sentence and write for ten minutes.

My relationship to sleep is...

Create a whimsical fantasy collage of where you would like to sleep. Glue it here. Look at it at night just before sleep.

Tips to help with sleep:

Keep yourself screen-free an hour before sleep.
No screen light for your brain.

Write in a notebook to empty your head
of any thoughts from the day.

Make your bed a beautiful place to sleep.
Comfy pillows, clean sheets, a bed made to welcome you.

Create a nightly ritual to help yourself sleep.
Do the same few things every single night
to help yourself prepare for bed.

Look at your sleep image.

Listen to a
sleep meditation.

BONUS TIP! When you travel, bring the things you need to help you sleep, such as a sleep mask, a pillowcase from home, something to read before bed, a sleep meditation.

What can you do to help yourself with your sleep?

BOUNDARY CARD:

It may feel selfish to take care of yourself, love yourself, and do things that are good for you. It is not selfish.

Caring for Your Body

Your body is your home. It needs care and attention to feel well. Your body needs support with rest, food, movement, cleaning, dressing, and safety from harm. Those basics can be done mindfully or mindlessly. Try staying aware when you are caring for your body so you can be attentive to yourself.

Your body is also a boundary, a physical space that is only for you.

Write a letter to your body acknowledging how you have treated it.

Move Like a Child

Moving your body is part of your self-care foundation. You are designed to be active and moving.

 Make a list of one hundred physical things you enjoyed doing as a child.

1. _____
2. _____
3. _____
4. _____
5. _____
6. _____
7. _____
8. _____
9. _____
10. _____
11. _____
12. _____
13. _____
14. _____
15. _____
16. _____
17. _____
18. _____
19. _____
20. _____
21. _____

22. _____
23. _____
24. _____
25. _____
26. _____
27. _____
28. _____
29. _____
30. _____
31. _____
32. _____
33. _____
34. _____
35. _____
36. _____
37. _____
38. _____
39. _____
40. _____
41. _____
42. _____

43. _____
44. _____
45. _____
46. _____
47. _____
48. _____
49. _____
50. _____
51. _____
52. _____
53. _____
54. _____
55. _____
56. _____
57. _____
58. _____
59. _____
60. _____
61. _____
62. _____
63. _____
64. _____
65. _____
66. _____
67. _____
68. _____
69. _____
70. _____
71. _____

72. _____
73. _____
74. _____
75. _____
76. _____
77. _____
78. _____
79. _____
80. _____
81. _____
82. _____
83. _____
84. _____
85. _____
86. _____
87. _____
88. _____
89. _____
90. _____
91. _____
92. _____
93. _____
94. _____
95. _____
96. _____
97. _____
98. _____
99. _____
100. _____

Write a list of the movement you like to do now as an adult.

⌂ BOUNDARY CARD:

Every day you get chances to say Yes and No. Pay attention and practice, practice, practice.

Your boundaries get stronger by using them.

How do you, or can you, make movement part of your daily routine? What will work for you?

Give Your Body Attention

Movement needs to be on your calendar like any other appointment you have. This is an appointment with yourself.

Dance freestyle with the music turned up.

Taking an exercise class helps because it meets at a certain time and someone else plans what you will do.

If you haven't been moving for a while or are trying something new, it helps to get a coach or trainer or a friend to join you.

Don't do it to "lose weight." Do it to feel good in your body.

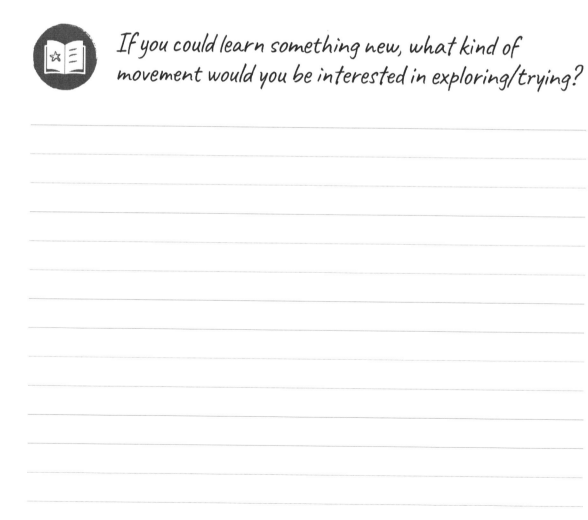

If you could learn something new, what kind of movement would you be interested in exploring/trying?

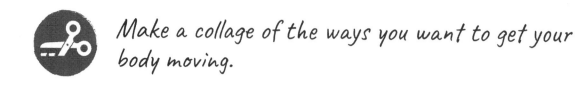

Make a collage of the ways you want to get your body moving.

If you have an injury or health issue, your body needs your extra **attention, help** and **support**.

 Describe any injuries or health issues and how they have changed you.

 Part 1: *Allow your body to write you a letter. Your body will tell you how you've been treating it when it is injured and unwell. Your body will ask you to treat it better.*

Dear You, You have been the one in charge and you've...

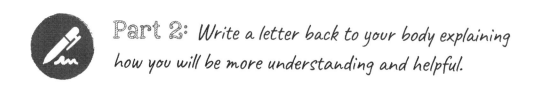

Part 2: Write a letter back to your body explaining how you will be more understanding and helpful.

Dear Gorgeous, Useful, Fabulous Body,

Magic Power of Boundaries

I can say yes.

I can say no.

I can change my mind.

I can trust myself.

I can choose a new path.

I can make changes to my life.

Boundaries are not feelings.

I can use my boundaries to take care of me.

It's OK if someone doesn't like my boundary.

Self-care is required to have healthy boundaries.

Self-care is important for me.

My boundaries don't come from other people.

Use one of the Magic Powers of Boundaries above as a journal prompt and write for ten minutes.

Archetypes & Boundaries

Archetypes are patterns, stories, character types that move through our lives. You will recognize ones that show up in your life. You can learn many things from an archetype.

Here are some archetypes you may recognize:

 Workaholic: *Busy, works and works, no time to play*

 Caretaker: *Takes care of everything and everyone*

 Lover: *Chases after love in all the wrong places*

 Numb-Er: *Doesn't want to feel things;*
Alchemist with feelings through numbing

 Isolator: *So lonely it makes you want to scream,*
but no one can hear the scream

 Protector: *Keeps lots of secrets, hides the truth*

 Sacrificer: *Gives up self for the needs for others*
(also true for caretaker and lover too)

One or more of these seven patterns, or archetypes,
show up in nearly everyone.
To learn more about each of these,
please read my book **Transform Your Boundaries**.

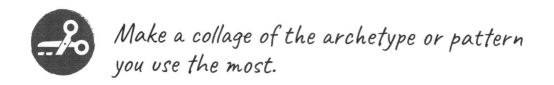

Make a collage of the archetype or pattern you use the most.

After you make your collage, write about what you notice in your collage. Ask this archetype some questions.

What can I learn from you about self-care?

_____

_____

_____

_____

_____

_____

_____

_____

What boundaries do I need to practice to not be consumed by you?

_____

_____

_____

_____

_____

_____

_____

_____

_____

_____
_____
_____
_____
_____
_____
_____
_____
_____
_____
_____
_____

Other Archetypes

Here are some other archetypes, patterns, or big energies you may notice moving through your life. Looking at your self-care and boundaries around these archetypes can help you grow.

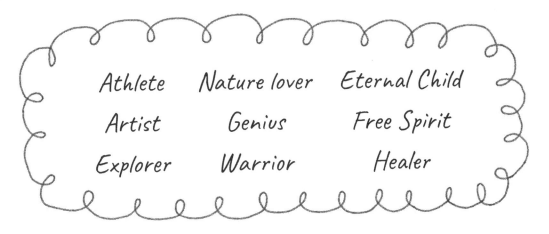

Athlete   Nature lover   Eternal Child

Artist   Genius   Free Spirit

Explorer   Warrior   Healer

There are many more archetypes. You can find lists of archetypes online. Pick the ones that show up in your life.

Feelings

Setting boundaries always brings up feelings. You may have feelings about your Yes and No. Other people may have feelings about your Yes and No.

Feelings just want to be understood.

Journaling is a useful way to listen to your feelings. If you make time to understand your feelings, it helps you accept your true feelings. Your feelings pile up inside if you ignore them. Ignoring your feelings will make you feel terrible.

Art may also be a way to express your feelings.

The feelings I ignored or stuffed down...

Right now I am feeling...because...

(You probably have more than one feeling. Write about more than one.)

The feeling that comes up with my boundary is...

⬆ BOUNDARY CARD:

It is your responsibility to mind your own boundary.

Listening to Your Owl

Listening to your compass is essential to figuring out what you need in your life. Your compass gives you direction in your life. Your compass is like a wise owl. You can ask your inner compass/owl anything.

Write down a question you want to ask your compass, your inner owl, your wise self.

Question: _____

_____

_____

_____

Let your compass, your deep truth and wisdom write you an answer to the question.

Dear _____ (your name), This is my truth about your question...

_____

_____

_____

_____

_____

Read what your wise compass wrote.
What is the Yes/No direction you were given?

Use this method of letting your compass write you a letter any time you need.

Permission to Say Yes or No

In order to listen to your compass, your Yes and No, your truth, your owl, you need to give yourself permission to listen to your compass.

 Try this when you have a boundary issue come up. Someone asks or invites you to do something, and it requires you to figure out if that is a Yes or No for you

 Part 1: What does my compass say about this issue? What is my truth?

_____

_____

_____

_____

_____

_____

_____

_____

_____

_____

_____

_____

Part 2: Write yourself a permission note using the sentences below.

Today, I give myself permission to say yes to...

Today I give myself permission to say no to...

Who

Your boundaries have one job and that job is to take care of you.

 ## Make a list of the people in your life with whom you would like to have better boundaries.

(Don't say "everyone." Be specific, make a list, write their names down below.)

I want new and better boundaries with:

Working Through a Boundary Issue

*This is a guide to help you decide
what boundary you need in a situation.*

1. ## Who:
   Who is the person or the people I need to clarify my boundaries with?

2. ## Issue:
   *This is where you describe the issue you are having with someone or
   in a situation.*

3. ## What:
   *What does my compass say? What is a Yes for me and what is a
   No for me in this situation?*

4. ## Possible Consequences:
   What are the possible consequences for clarifying my boundary?

5. ## Pushback:
   *Pushback may be a negative response you get.
   What pushback can I expect?*

6. ## Self-care:
   How will setting this boundary take care of me?

7. ## Feelings:
   *How do I feel about clarifying this boundary? How can I take care
   of the feelings this brings up?*

Other People's Feelings

When someone else has feelings about your boundaries, it is up to them to take care of their own feelings.

 I am not able to make people feel certain feelings. I do not have that kind of power. If I did have that power...

Be a Boundary Builder

 Make a collage about the part of you that is working on boundaries.

We will call this part of you **The Boundary Builder.** What does this part of you look like? Use only three to four images in your collage.

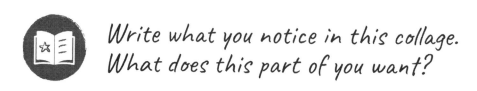

Write what you notice in this collage.
What does this part of you want?

This part of me wants...

This part of me is tired of...

This part of me is ready for...

Right now I need to:

☐ Work through an issue
☐ Schedule my self-care
☐ Do self-care
☐ Give myself permission
☐ Review boundary lessons
☐ Revise my self-care wheel
☐ Journal about my feelings
☐ Stop shutting off messages from my body

 I realize...

Boundary Challengers

When you are dealing with an extreme boundary challenge — death, trauma, health issue, authority, wealth, mental health issue, addiction, or stress — it may feel much harder to have boundaries. It may feel like you are dealing with an angry bear. It may feel like your boundaries have collapsed and a wild bear is tearing you apart.

When you experience an extreme boundary challenge or extreme boundary challenger, what boundaries do you feel you have lost control over?

Rebuilding Boundaries

Though you may have lost control of the boundaries during an extreme challenge, that is what happens to all of us. Here are some journal prompts to help steer you back to the boundaries that are necessary during an extreme challenge or bear attack.

What are you responsible for and not responsible for?

What are your financial boundaries during this challenge?

How can you protect your time and access to you to take a break from the challenge?

How can you increase your self-care during this challenge?

Values & Boundaries

Boundaries and values are part of every culture, every family, and every community. Some boundaries may feel healthy and help us connect and support each other. Other boundaries or values may feel harmful. You may need to clarify your boundaries to protect yourself from the harmful or toxic aspects of a family, community, or culture.

In the family and culture I grew up in, I noticed...

My values are different from my family's...

_____

_____

_____

_____

_____

_____

_____

_____

_____

_____

_____

_____

_____

_____

_____

_____

_____

_____

_____

⬆ BOUNDARY CARD:

> *Resentment means you*
> *want to say No.*

The grief I have about the toxic culture...

Digital Diet

Wow, our lives online can consume us.

Taking a complete break, a digital detox, helps us think about where we want our boundaries. Step fully away from the online world for two to three days. Remind yourself or discover the wonder of digital-free spaces.

Only do these journal prompts AFTER you have had a digital detox.

My online presence is...

_____

_____

_____

_____

_____

_____

_____

_____

_____

_____

_____

_____

_____

_____

My privacy is...

The new digital boundaries I want are...

Stages of Boundary Expertise

Stages of Becoming a Boundaries Expert in Your Life and Becoming True to Who You Are

A. Do your self-care daily and do more when you have a challenge or need more

B. Speak your truth

C. Create clear agreements and contracts with people in your life

D. Stop saying, "I don't have time"

E. Ask others about their boundaries

F. Deal with tricky boundary situations without gossiping and drama

G. Create digital boundaries for yourself

A Grateful Heart

 Every day, do this one thing. Write down three things each day you are grateful for.

Just three.

Every single day.

1. _____

2. _____

3. _____

Research shows this could make you happier because you train your mind to notice the gifts from gratitude.

Revisiting the Journal Prompts

These are all of the Journal Prompts from inside The Mystery of Knowing Journal.
I recommend visiting these prompts again. Each time you go through them, you may notice different things about yourself. The words you write will change. You will get new insights. At any time you can read this list, write the Journal Prompt (JP) at the top of a fresh sheet of paper, and write for ten to fifteen minutes.

Use the same journal process every time you write:

Write ten to fifteen minutes, **Read** what you wrote, **Reflect**, and Write for one to two minutes about your writing.

1. As fast you can, write a list of reasons why you want to be more connected to your authentic voice.

2. Where and when do you feel your authentic self is hidden, buried, or covered?

3. Write a letter to your hidden self. Dear Hidden Self,

4. Who in your life, now or in the past, accepts you as you are and encourages you to be authentic?

5. In what ways are you courageous? What courageous things have you done?

6. My fear about being authentic is:

7. Write some kind things you can say to yourself when you are hurting.

8. Make a collage (using only two to three images) of a Compassionate Being who is going to live in your heart.

9. Finish these sentences after you make your Compassionate Being:

   I want you to know, you are...

   I see...

   My words for you are...

   Trust...

   When you are hurting in your heart...

10. How well do you listen to your true Yes and No? When is it easy to listen? What makes it hard?

11. Make a bubble brainstorm of all the "Shoulds" you hear in your head.

12. Write some kind things you can say to yourself when you are hurting. (When you are really hurting or upset, return to this JP.) Then read the words aloud to yourself.

13. Every year starting in January, make a new self-care wheel. See what changes for you from year to year. Notice what you seem to master.

14. How can you wake from hibernation like the bear? What are your self-care needs that it is time to wake up to?

15. Is self-care part of your daily plan?

16. Writing as fast as you can, make a list of fifty fun things you would do if you had more time. (Pretend that money does not matter—list all the fun things you would like to do.) It's OK if you repeat yourself.

17. Write some baby steps you can take now to help you get closer to these fun things.

    I can try baby stepping with...

18. Starfish sometimes cling to things in the water. What could you stop clinging to that wastes your time?

19. My relationship to sleep is...

20. What can you do to help yourself with your sleep?

21. Write a letter to your body acknowledging how you have treated it.

22. Make a list of one hundred physical things you enjoyed doing as a child.

23. Write a list of the movement you like to do now as an adult.

24. How do you, or can you, make movement part of your daily routine? What will work for you?

25. If you could learn something new, what kind of movement would you be interested in exploring/trying?

26. Describe any injuries or health issues and how they have changed you.

    Part 1: Allow your body to write you a letter. Your body will tell you how you've been treating it when it is injured and unwell. Your body will ask you to treat it better.

    Part 2: Write a letter back to your body explaining how you will be more understanding and helpful.

27. Use one of the Magic Powers of Boundaries (page 74) as a journal prompt and write for ten minutes.

28. Use one of the seven archetypes. What can I learn from you about self-care? What boundaries do I need to practice to not be consumed by you?

29. The feelings I ignored, stuffed...

30. Right now I am feeling...because...(You probably have more than one feeling.)

31. Write down a question you want to ask your compass, your owl, your wise self.
    Question:

32. Let your compass, your deep truth, and wisdom write you an answer to the question.
    Dear ____(your name), This is my truth about your question...

33. Read what your wise self wrote. What is the Yes/No direction you were given?

34. The feeling that comes up with shifting my boundary is...
    Part 1: What does my compass say about this issue? What is my truth?
    Part 2: Write yourself a permission note using the sentences below.

35. Today, I give myself permission to say yes to...

36. Today I give myself permission to say no to...

37. Make a list of the people in your life with whom you would like better boundaries. (Don't say "everyone." Be specific, make a list, write their names down below.)
    I want new and better boundaries with:

38. This is a guide to help you decide what boundary you need in a situation.

    Who: Who is the person or the people I need to clarify my boundaries with?

    Issue: This is where you describe the issue you are having with someone or in a situation.

    What: What does your compass say? What is a Yes for me and what is a No for me in this situation?

    Possible Consequences: What are the possible consequences for clarifying my boundary?

    Pushback: Pushback may be a negative response you get. What pushback can I expect?

    Self-care: How will setting this boundary take care of me?

    Feelings: How do I feel about clarifying this boundary? How can I take care of the feelings this brings up?

39. I am not able to make people feel certain feelings. I do not have that kind of power. If I did have that power...

40. The One who wants boundaries. What does this part of you want?

    This part of me wants...

    This part of me is tired of...This part of me is ready for...

    I realize...

41. When you experience an extreme boundary challenge or extreme boundary challenger, or angry bear, what boundaries do you feel you have lost control over?

42. What are you responsible for and not responsible for?

43. What are your financial boundaries during this challenge?

44. How can you protect your time and access to you to take a break from the challenge?

45. How can you increase your self-care during this challenge?

46. In the family and culture I grew up in, I noticed...

    My values are different than my family's...

    The grief I have about the toxic culture...

47. My online presence is...

    My privacy is...

    The new digital boundaries I want are...

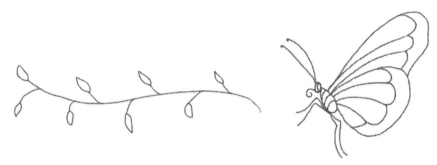

Bonus Journal Prompts

By now you are probably much better at journaling.
In case you want more prompts, try these.

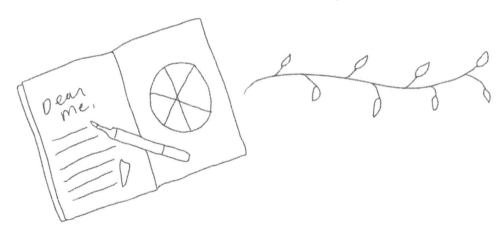

Write a list of the things you do that make you feel more connected to yourself.

I can get out of balance when...

These are the places that feed my soul...

It is not selfish when I...

When I get afraid of appearing selfish because I take care of myself, I can reassure myself by saying this...

It is my job to really pay attention to my boundaries when I am...

The thing I really need to say Yes to is...

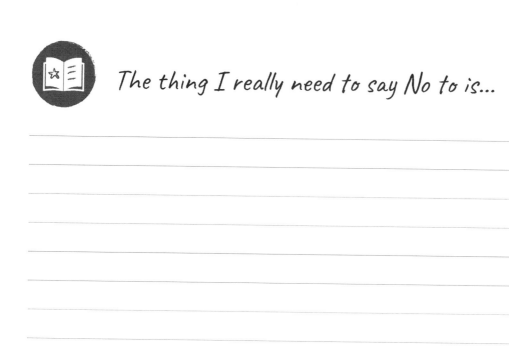

The thing I really need to say No to is...

I really appreciate my boundaries because...

It's hard to watch someone who doesn't let themselves have boundaries. I sometimes wish I could give my boundaries to...

I need to seriously schedule my time differently to allow myself...

I wish other people would stop asking me to...

When my boundary gets pushed on, I...

I need to be more firm holding my boundary when...

I feel manipulated when...

I am going to protect myself from manipulation by...

I tried to have a boundary and it collapsed.
I want to rebuild this boundary...

A very pushy person in my life is...

The boundary to help me around pushy people is...

To create calm and peace in my life, I am willing to...

I trust myself to make my decisions about...

I am going to pay more attention to my inner compass, Yes and No, because...

The feelings that are hard for me are...

The feeling I keep running from is...

The feeling I want to get to know better is...

This is how I will pay attention to what I am feeling...

The big messy thing in my life is...

I lost my boundaries in the big messy thing when...

I am going to let myself have boundaries even in the big messy thing by...

I am on overload from...

I am willing to reduce some of my load by...

The boundaries that will help me with overload are...

I am giving more than I have...

Sometimes the expectations I have for myself feel unrealistic...

The boundary I can use when I am unrealistic is...

I demand too much of myself because...

I want to speak my truth about...

I need to give myself permission to...

Listening to my intuition is...

Meditation is...

I draw strength from...

Make a collage of images that give you strength.

My boundaries can support my recovery and healing in the following ways:

Write a list of boundaries you would like for yourself with social media.

Who in your life would you like to have boundary conversations with, to support each other as you strengthen your boundaries?

I am curious about the boundaries of (a friend, mentor, colleague). Who did you pick and why?

In a world that has very little privacy,
I am allowed to...

Signs of my own depletion are...

When I am depleted, I can nourish myself by...

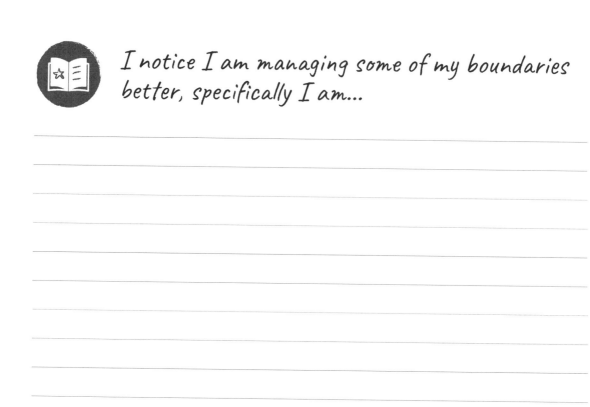

I notice I am managing some of my boundaries better, specifically I am...

I get these signals from my body when I need to stop pushing myself...

These are my body signals I want to pay more attention to...

I could notice the boundaries of others better by...

Describe a big change in your life that is forcing a big change of your boundaries.

Something I have ignored for a long time is...

The days of the week that I am off are...

Sometimes it is hard to protect my time off...

The boundaries in the culture around me are changing, and I notice...

I have ignored this issue because setting a boundary could mean...

I set a boundary and the person
responded with...

Socially, these are the people who are a priority for me to spend time with, and I make efforts to connect...

I am ready for a new experience or adventure and would like to...

I may be giving too much of myself away to...

In my work, I feel out of balance with... and need to reset by...

I have been numbing out by... and think it would be better if I...

I can pay better attention to managing my money by...

This is what I learned about money and spending growing up...

My goals and boundaries with money I need to practice are...

My greatest boundary teacher right now is...

What do you remember about asserting your boundaries as a child or teenager?

I can see the following improvements in my self-care...

I am making more time to appreciate...

I can practice slowing down...

The chaos I want to be free from is....

The stuff I no longer need is...

I can go easier on myself when it comes to...
I tend to overdo...

Some of my agreements need more clarity around expectations and roles. I would like more clarity with...

I am feeling hopeful about...

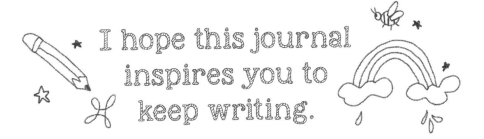

I hope this journal
inspires you to
keep writing.

Please note in my books *Transform Your Boundaries*
and *Naming and Taming Overwhelm*, both have questions
to use for journaling at the end of each chapter.

I am a lifelong journaler who believes the art
of reflecting is the way to our deeper knowing.

Please visit my website at sarrigilman.com and follow
me on social media for more insights and workshops.

Acknowledgments

I want to thank those who inspire me as I guide people to the practice of journaling:

Kay Adams: *Center for Journal Therapy*

Kim Krans: *The Wild Unknown Animal Spirit Deck and Guidebook, and The Wild Unknown Archetypes and Guidebook*

Seena B. Frost: *SoulCollage®*

Caroline Myss: *Archetype Cards*

James Pennebaker: *Writing to Heal*

Isabel Allende: *Paula*

Patricia Donegan: *Haiku Mind*

Kristin Neff & Christopher Germer: *The Mindful Self-Compassion Workbook*

And to all the wonderful books I read where a diary or journal appeared. Many thanks for the blank journals I was gifted — each one has been a companion.

Made in the USA
Middletown, DE
26 September 2020